CURTIS INTERNATIONAL
PORTRAITS OF GREATNESS

•

General Editor
Dr. Enzo Orlandi

Text by
Cesare Giardini

Translator
Frances Lanza

Published by

ARNOLDO MONDADORI EDITORE
and

THE CURTIS PUBLISHING COMPANY

THE
LIFE
&
TIMES
OF
COLUMBUS

CP

CURTIS BOOKS
A division of
The Curtis Publishing Company
Philadelphia • New York

A MAN OF DIVINE PROVIDENCE?

Below: One of the many depictions of the landing of Columbus, stressing the Christian spirit of the enterprise. Christopher Columbus was convinced that his name predestined him to be, like his patron saint, a "Christ-bearer." This is the meaning of the words "Xpo FERENS" in his somewhat enigmatic signature, which has been much discussed by scholars.

Among the many biographies of Columbus there is a recurring theme of what we might call "divine providence." In his own writings Columbus returns over and over again to the idea that God put into his mind the conviction that it was possible to sail all the way to the Indies. "An obvious miracle," he writes in the preface to the *Libro de las profecias*, "meant to ensure the success of such a great voyage." Indeed the life of the discoverer abounds in episodes in which an acute observer may see evidence of a will external and superior to his, or, in other words, divine. Often it is a matter of coincidence, but to Columbus every coincidence was significant. He was a mystic—not, to be sure, a saint, but certainly an inspired spirit. The enthusiasm he put into everything he did derived from the intensity of his spiritual life. Queen Isabella of Spain and Christopher Columbus were born in the same year, 1451, the former on April 22 at Madrigal de Las Altas Torres and the latter in Genoa between August and October. Fate seems sometimes to delight in making strange combinations among the pieces of the game it plays through the centuries. If it could be further proved, as some historians would have it, that Amerigo Vespucci was born in the same year, the coincidence would be even stranger. The three protagonists of the great oceanic adventure destined to change the face of the world—the discoverer, his noble patron and the man from whom the new world was to take its name—were all born in the first year of the second half of that 15th century, which was to open a new period of history.

Right: Christopher Columbus in the New World, *a fresco by Carlone. Far right: Christopher Columbus. This mosaic by Antonio Salviati is in the Palazzo Tursi in Genoa, the town where the discoverer was born and to which he always felt a patriot's loyalty.*

*Above: Genoa in 1481,
in a painting by Cristoforo
Grassi. Left: An etching
of Genoa in 1486.
Right: The stone
commemorative of Columbus
on the house where
he was supposedly born. The
Genoese were highly
appreciated in Portugal
as men versed in navigation.
Their excessive individualism
was one of the reasons for the
decay of the Republic of Genoa.
On the other hand, the energy
and persistence of their individual
efforts made the Genoese
powerful in the world of finance.*

GENOA WAS IN DECAY, BUT THE GENOESE WERE EVERYWHERE

Christopher Columbus was born in the Olivella district of Genoa, near the gate of the same name, of which his father, Domenico, a simple wool weaver, was the warder. The city, at this time, was quite different from what it had been in the 13th and 14th centuries, when so many brave navigators had set out from its port to sail over unknown seas. Historians have settled on 1475 as the last year of the prestige and power of the Genoese Republic. In that year, when its colonies in Crimea fell into the hands of the Turks, the empire of Genoa became a thing of the past. The reasons for this decay were numerous and complex; first among them, perhaps, the quarrels among the great families, which periodically covered the streets of the city with blood. In the six years between 1390 and 1396 there were at least 11 revolutions and 11 successive doges on the throne, one of whom reigned for only two days. With the Turks in Asia Minor and the Balkans, the Mediterranean situation was becoming more and more thorny and uncertain. Yet Genoa's great rival, Venice, because of its justly celebrated political wisdom, managed to maintain its position. Further, the Genoese had taught the science of navigation, of which they were past masters, to the Catalonians, the Castilians, the Portuguese, the English, the French and even to the Turks and the Persians. In so doing, they had raised up rivals on the sea over which they had so long ruled supreme. Nevertheless, even after the loss of their Mediterranean empire, there was a period in which the Genoese were to be found everywhere, as indispensable elements in the fields of finance and commerce. Genoese migrants were no longer, as in the Middle Ages, sailors and whalers; they were bankers and shipbuilders, looking for chances to invest their money. Many of them were in Spain. And later, when their fellow citizen, Columbus, had opened the route to the West Indies, they played an important part in the colonization and exploitation of the new lands.

The "Catholic sovereigns" who furnished Columbus with the means of achieving his great sea voyage. Below: Ferdinand of Aragon with his son, Don Juan—a detail from The Madonna of the Catholic Kings, *from a painting of the Hispano-Flemish School. Opposite:* Portrait of Isabella of Castile *by Bartolomé Bermejo. Isabella, the daughter of John II, who died in 1454, was declared in 1468 heir to the throne of Castile. A year later she married Ferdinand of Aragon, but she had to combat the opposition of her brother, Henry IV, and that of Alfonso V of Portugal before obtaining recognition of her rights.*

"A MONARCH, AN EMPIRE AND A SWORD"

While Genoa decayed, Spain was rapidly expanding. It was preparing to go beyond the divisions and disorders of the Middle Ages, to become first a united nation and then a major European power, ruling over an empire on which the sun would never set. Hernando de Acuña, the favorite poet of Charles V, summed up the elements that made for the greatness of Spain in these words: "a monarch, an empire and a sword." This grandeur endured for nearly a century, from the accession to the throne of Ferdinand of Aragon and Isabella of Castile in 1474 to the disastrous defeat of Philip II's "Invincible Armada" at the hands of the English in 1588. Spain's most glorious moment was during the "Catholic Sovereigns'" joint reign. In these years Spanish power swelled and, indeed, overflowed.

Spain, particularly Castile, under the rule of such weak and inept kings as Henry IV, Isabella's older brother, had gone through a period of degradation. With the advent of Ferdinand and Isabella there was a radical change. The 40 years of their reign (Isabella died in 1504 and Ferdinand in 1516) made Spain into a new nation. The great events of this period were the following: the submission of the turbulent nobility and the resulting consolidation of the throne; the union of the crowns of Aragon and Castile, voted by the Cortes in Toledo shortly after the birth of an heir, Don Juan; the victory over Spain's traditional enemy, Portugal (1479); the victorious 10-year battle for Granada (1482–1492), which ended a struggle that had gone on for centuries to wrest the country from the Moors; the recovery of Roussillon (1493); the annexation of Navarre (1511); the reconquest of Naples (1503); the beginning, by virtue of the occupation of Oran, of the conquest of North Africa. What further accomplishment—human or superhuman, as another historian asks—could be expected? Nothing more—or less—than the conquest of a new world. Obviously Columbus came along at the psychological moment.

"MY HEART IS ALWAYS IN GENOA"

"The glory of Columbus is a glory of Italy and of the whole world, exclusive of the Spaniards, who did nothing but torment him and exploit his discovery in a most barbarous and wicked manner, by turning it into a piratical enterprise." Thus, with a rare sense of balance, writes the Spaniard Menéndez y Pelayo.

No one possessed of common sense any longer believes the often clever and apparently learned arguments that have been mustered at various times to endow Columbus with a nationality other than Italian and to describe him as an unscrupulous adventurer, a pirate or worse. There is a document, universally recognized as being by his own hand, in which, on February 22, 1498, in Seville, shortly before setting out on his third voyage, he instructed his heirs as to the disposition of his property. Its importance lies in the fact that the "Admiral," as he signed himself from the time of his landing on the far shore of the "Ocean Sea," spoke of himself as "born in Genoa" and went on to say that he had gone from that city to Castile to serve Their Highnesses Ferdinand and Isabella. In evidence of his attachment to his native city, he ordered his son, Don Diego, to set up a fund at the Genoese Bank of Saint George, which should serve to relieve the poor of taxes. In 1502, shortly before the fourth voyage, it was to the same Bank of Saint George that Columbus sent documents and copies of documents relative to the privileges conferred upon him by the Spanish King and Queen. The bearer was Nicolò Olderigo, Genoese ambassador to Spain. It is clear that Genoa was always in his mind. "Noble gentlemen," he said in his letter to the bank, "although my body is here, my heart is always there."

Left: An old print of the house at Cogoleto, formerly thought to have belonged to the Columbus family. Below: A view of Savona at the end of the 15th century. Domenico Colombo, the explorer's father, went to live there in 1470, having bought a tavern and begun to trade in cheese and wine. At the same time he continued to practice, quite unprofitably, the trade of weaving, in Genoa. Christopher, the first-born, had three brothers—one of whom died young—and one sister, who married a cheese merchant. The older of the two surviving brothers, Bartholomew, became Columbus's right-hand man. Diego, who was 17 years younger, likewise followed him to the New World. Antonio Gallo, secretary of the Bank of Saint George, wrote in 1506 that Christopher and Bartholomew, "as soon as they reached the age of puberty, went to sea, according to their family's custom."

AN EARLY LOVE OF THE SEA

Left: Chios at the end of the 15th century. This island was a Genoese colony until 1566, and Columbus went there in 1474, aboard the Roxana, *a four-masted vessel armed with 18 lombards and six mortars. We do not know in what capacity Columbus traveled, but he may have represented some Genoese mercantile establishment. Below: René II of Anjou. At the age of 22 Columbus was aboard one of his ships sent to capture the galleass* Fernandina *of Juan II, king of Aragon. Off the coast of Sardinia Columbus had to resort to a stratagem in order to pacify the crew.*

Records of the youth of Columbus are completely lacking. We can rely only on the book written by his son, Ferdinand, who took part in two of the voyages. But Ferdinand quite honestly confesses to a lack of information about his father's early years. Of one thing we can be sure: Columbus was drawn at an early age to the sea. In 1501 he wrote to Ferdinand and Isabella: "At a very tender age I became a sailor, and I have continued until this day. The art of navigation incites those who follow it to learn the secrets of the world. For 40 years I have followed this trade, and I have sailed all the navigable seas. . . ." If we count backward 40 years this would mean that Columbus first went to sea when he was nine or ten years old. Not at quite so young an age, but a very few years later he probably served on the merchant ships that went from port to port along the Ligurian coast. At the age of 22 we find him aboard an armed ship in the service of René d'Anjou, which was sent to capture a galleass belonging to Juan II of Aragon. Ferdinand quotes a lost letter from his father as saying: "Off the island of San Pietro near Sardinia, I was told that there were two ships and a carrack with the said galleass, which disturbed my people, and they resolved to go no further, but to sail right back to Marseilles and pick up another ship and more people. I, seeing that nothing could be done against the force of their wills without some stratagem, yielded to their desires; and then, *changing the feed of the compass needle*, made sail when night fell, and on the following day at sunup we found ourselves off Cape Carthage while all aboard were certain we were on our way to Marseilles." If this account is exact, it seems as if Columbus must have been the commanding officer. Historians give credit to the story and date it as of 1473. A year later Columbus sailed to the island of Chios, off the west coast of Asia Minor. After he had settled in Portugal, in 1476, it is probable that he traveled, in the service of its king, Alfonso V, down the coast of Africa as far as the Gulf of Guinea. But at this point we must pause to consider how Columbus came to Portugal. For this was a turning point in his life.

A MYSTERIOUS VOYAGE

It has been said that Columbus was wounded in a sea battle and swam to safety on the coast of Portugal on August 13, 1476. This is how it came about. In 1476 Genoa armed a squadron of ships to carry merchandise to northern Europe. The squadron was made up of three galleasses—the *Roxana*, the *Squarciafica* and the *Bettinella*—one whaler and a Flemish vessel, the *Bechalla*. The squadron sailed from Noli on May 31, rounded the Pillars of Hercules (Gibraltar) and, on August 13, was sailing along the coast of Portugal, between Cape Santa Maria and Cape St. Vincent. Here it was attacked by a group of some 15 Franco-Portuguese ships, under the command of a famous seaman, Guillaume de Casenove. Genoa was at peace with both Spain and Portugal, but the *Bechalla* was flying the flag of Burgundy, which was at war with France, and Casenove was attracted by the prospect of rich booty. The battle lasted 10 hours, and a Spanish chronicler writes that the Genoese fought "so valiantly that it was a thing of wonder." A fire broke out and spread from one ship to another; the French lost four vessels and the Genoese three, among them the *Bechalla*, which had Columbus aboard. Although wounded, Columbus managed to swim six miles to shore, landing at Lagos. There he was cared for by the inhabitants and sent on to Barcelona, where his younger brother, Bartholomew, was already living. From this same period dates also Columbus's adventurous voyage, aboard a Genoese ship, to Iceland and possibly even farther. "I sailed," he says, "a hundred leagues beyond the island of Tile (Thule) . . . and to this island, which is as big as England, come English, with their merchandise, especially those of Bristol." Thule had been visited by Pytheas, a navigator from Marseilles of the fourth century B.C., and was termed by Ptolemy the northernmost boundary of the known world. It was, in all probability, one of the Shetlands. However, it hardly corresponds to the description "as big as England." Rinaldo Caddeo thinks that Columbus's words should be read: "I sailed to *another* Tile. . . ." Not the Thule of Pytheas and Ptolemy, but almost certainly Iceland and perhaps even Greenland.

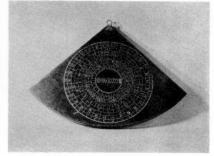

"OUR LORD REVEALED TO ME THAT IT WAS FEASIBLE"

The cosmography and geography of the 15th century had a great deal of the fairy tale about them; they were highly colored and filled with imagination. When Columbus set out on his bold voyage he had absorbed the culture of the age into which he had been born. He was by no means ignorant; it is probable that, like all self-taught men, he had read widely. He was familiar with such writers as Aristotle, Strabo, Ptolemy and also with such more recent books as the *Imago mundi* of Cardinal d'Ailly (the last great geographer in the Scholastic tradition), the *De sphaera mundi* of John of Holywood (both these dating from 1403) and the *Historia rerum ubique gestarum* of Pope Pius II (Piccolomini). From this last, he may have drawn his notions of Ptolemaic geography. He devoured, of course, the *Book of Ser Marco Polo*. That he meditated upon this book and made copious notes in the margins we know from the copy formerly in his possession, which is preserved in the Columbian Library of Seville. Columbus was the sort of reader who always has a pen or pencil in hand; all his books that have come down to us are similarly annotated. Besides instructing himself from books, he garnered all sorts of information on the subjects that interested him. In the letter that his son, Ferdinand, tells us he wrote to the Catholic Sovereigns in 1501, he says: "I have had dealings and conversation with learned men, priests and laymen, Latins and Greeks, Jews and Moors, and many others of other sects. I found Our Lord very favorable to this my desire, and to further it, He granted me the gift of knowledge. He made me skilled in seamanship, equipped me with the sciences of astronomy, geometry and arithmetic, and taught my mind and hand to draw this sphere and upon it the cities, rivers, mountains, islands and ports. . . . During this time I have made it my business to read all that has been written on geography, history, philosophy and other sciences. Then Our Lord revealed to me that it was feasible to sail from here to the Indies and placed in me a burning desire to carry out this plan. . . ."

16

Opposite page: A view of Lisbon from the Libro de grandezas de España *(1548) of Pedro Medina. The city was of Phoenician origin. It became a Roman town in the age of Augustus, then passed into the hands of the Germans, the Visigoths and the Arabs, to whom it belonged until it was conquered, in 1147, by Alfonso Henriques, the first king of Portugal. Above: Imaginary portrait of Marco Polo from the first printed edition of his book, made in Nuremberg. The three other illustrations on this page are from Codex 264 of the Bodleian Library of Oxford. Above, left: The Great Khan (emperor of China) riding out of the gate of the city of Shangtu (Coleridge's Xanadu) to go hunting. Below, left: The port of Zaitun. Below, right: Inhabitants of Yachi (the modern Kunming, on the Burma Road).*

17

Below: Planisphere of Paolo dal Pozzo Toscanelli. Columbus seems to have made use of a copy of a letter from this learned Florentine humanist and cosmographer to advance his cause. According to Toscanelli, there was a distance of about 5,000 nautical miles from Lisbon westward to "the great and noble city of Quinsay (King-sze)." This was the name by which Marco Polo knew the modern Hangchow, capital of the province of Chekiang. One of the things that most struck him about it was the presence of some 12,000 stone bridges, which must have reminded him of Venice. Right: Prince Henry the Navigator Consults the Cartographers, a painting by Sousa Lopez. Columbus made his first proposals to Alfonso V of Portugal, nephew of the navigator, renewing them later to Alfonso's son, João II. Alfonso, because he had just emerged from a disastrous war against Spain (1479), turned him down, and João, who was intent upon an eastward route, could not make up his mind.

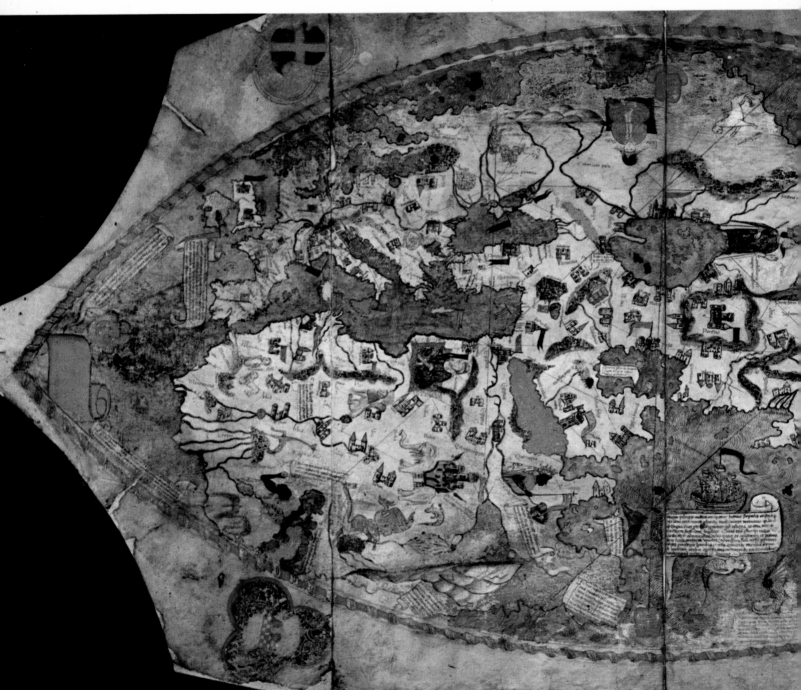

A SCANDALOUS IDEA

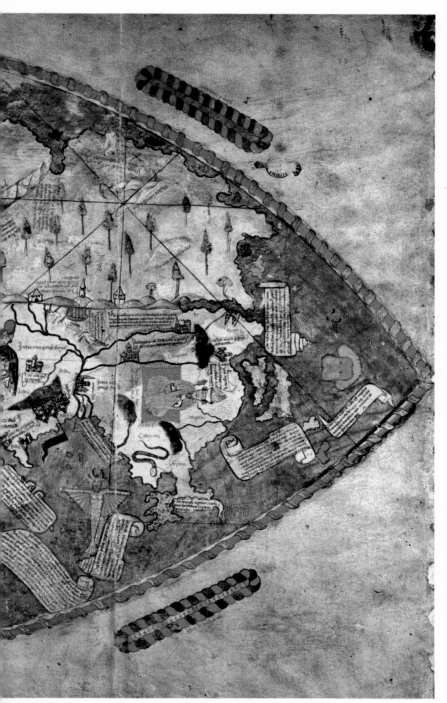

It was probably during the early years he spent in Lisbon that Columbus was struck by the idea that it would be possible to sail from "these parts"—that is, the west coast of the Iberian Peninsula—to "the Indies." The Portuguese, under the guidance of Prince Henry the Navigator, were groping for a route along the coast of Africa. Columbus's idea of sailing west was startling, and even scandalous. The 10 years (1476–1486) that Columbus spent in Portugal, mostly in Lisbon, where there were many Genoese, were happy ones. He made charts and undertook several voyages—one of them, in 1478, to Genoa—and also took a wife. He married Doña Felipa Perestrello y Moniz, whose father's family came from Piacenza in Italy and who was related, through her mother, to the royal house of Bragança. He enjoyed a good reputation both as a seaman and as a chartmaker, and looked after the interests of several important Genoese merchants. Within a few years he might have become a rich man. But he was fired with a passion for exploration, and everything in his surroundings conspired to feed this flame. His wife's father, Bartholomew Perestrello, had rediscovered Madeira and the islands adjoining it (originally discovered by 14th-century Italians) and had been given the title of Captain of Porto Santo. His mother-in-law, Isabel Moniz, turned over to him all her husband's nautical maps. Later, Columbus and his wife went to live at Porto Santo (30 miles northeast of Madeira), and there, surrounded by the Atlantic, all the myths and mirages of the great ocean rose up to assail him. But in order to achieve his dream he needed the support of a king. Meanwhile his private life and the life of his time were eventful. In 1480—or perhaps the year after—his son, Diego, was born. In 1481 King Alfonso V died, and soon after this, perhaps in 1483, Columbus lost his wife. He went back to Lisbon and tried his luck in vain with João II, Alfonso's successor. In 1485 this king's maritime commission rejected Columbus's project. The only hope left to him was Spain.

SYMPATHY AND HELP AT THE MONASTERY OF LA RÁBIDA

Opposite: B. Mercadé's painting, Columbus at the Gate of the Monastery of La Rábida (*Gerona, Provincial Archaeological Museum*). *Below:* Columbus with His Son Diego at the Monastery of La Rábida *by Delacroix* (*Washington, D.C., National Gallery of Art, Chester Dale Collection*). *Bottom, left:* Columbus with His Sons Diego and Ferdinand *in an old Spanish painting. Bottom, right: Panel from one of the doors of the Capitol, Washington, D.C., by the sculptor Randolph Rogers. The scene is* The Departure of Columbus from La Rábida for the Court of Spain. *Randolph Rogers (1825–1892) was a pupil, in Florence, of Bartolini.*

Palos and La Rábida are fateful place names in the dramatic life of Columbus. The whitewashed monastery of La Rábida, shaded by a few trees, rises on the hills overlooking the Rio Tinto, a few miles from Palos de la Frontera. Columbus arrived there with a five-year-old child. In this southernmost region of Spain summer (the season of Columbus's arrival) is extremely hot, and little Diego was tired and thirsty. A recent biographer, Samuel Eliot Morison, says that Columbus must have been looking for a place where he could leave his son, since the Franciscans often "conducted schools for young boys." Columbus knocked at the monastery door, and from then on we have a series of fateful coincidences. Columbus was welcomed by the prior, Fra Juan Pérez, a former confessor of Queen Isabella, to whom he spoke freely of his great purpose and the disappointment with which he had met in Portugal. He had a chance, also, to talk to another monk, Antonio Marchena, a superior of the Franciscans in the sub-province of Seville and an astronomer. Both of them listened to him sympathetically. Other men skilled in navigation apparently frequented the monastery: a doctor, García Hernández; a pilot, Sebastiano Rodriguez, and a shipowner, Alonso Pinzón. Together they arranged for Columbus to go to Seville, leaving Diego in the monks' charge, and recommended him to Don Luis de la Cerda, Duke of Medina Celi, a grandee and shipbuilder. There were in Seville, as in many other Spanish cities, many Italians who enjoyed great esteem, and one of these, a Florentine banker named Berardi, offered Columbus friendship and aid. Medina Celi was fired with enthusiasm for the enterprise, and soon Columbus found himself about to get from him the "three or four well-equipped caravels" that he had said he needed. But a voyage so ambitious might have led to trouble with Portugal and hence required governmental backing. This was Isabella's answer when Medina Celi told her that he wished to sponsor the expedition. Let his protégé come to Cordova, she said, and she would take care of him herself. And so Columbus set out, hopefully, to the royal city.

THE WILY
KING FERDINAND

Auda no la
ei urtec tā Gar
erregue jau Fe
en bean bzc
foruac ta eu

Machiavelli studied attentively the career of Ferdinand of Aragon, the Catholic Sovereign, and went so far as to call him "the first king of Christendom." And the 16th-century Florentine historian, Guicciardini, passed the following laudatory judgment upon him: "What a difference there was between this prince's words and his deeds, and with what wiliness and secrecy he laid his plans!" Ferdinand himself was the first to brag of his ability to deceive: "The king of France," he says, "complains that I have twice deceived him. The idiot is lying. I've deceived him a dozen times or more." Below: Francisco de Mendete's painting, Ferdinand Pledges the "Fueros" at Bilbao (*the constitution of Biscay*).

THE DECISIVE ENCOUNTER
WITH QUEEN ISABELLA

After years of waiting in Portugal came the meeting—decisive for Columbus and his plans—with Queen Isabella. Louis Pfandl, a specialist in this period of Spanish history, says that the queen's features were "decidedly masculine," while those of her husband "might have belonged to a woman." Isabella was, indeed, a sort of "woman on horseback." Ferdinand was not inclined to back the oceanic adventure, but the queen was attracted by the idea of "attempting this great leap over the sea." She was particularly enthused by the idea that there were so many souls to be converted to the true religion. Isabella and Columbus understood each other. Both of them, at this time when they had attained maturity, had the same half-mystical, half-practical nature. They indulged in flights of imagination, but at the same time they kept their feet firmly on the ground. Columbus was every bit as religious as the queen. His son Ferdinand tells us that "he was so strict in matters of religion that, for fasting and saying prayers, he might have been

taken for a member of a religious order." Obviously this made for a strong bond between him and Isabella. But at the beginning of their acquaintance things did not go smoothly. When Columbus addressed himself to her for the first time, Isabella was deeply involved with the three-year-old war against Granada. The war against Granada was *her* war. For the 10 years of its duration, a chronicler tells us, "the queen dedicated all her thoughts and energy to obtaining money for its prosecution." This war, she hoped, would channel the energies of the turbulent Spanish nobility into heroic and useful deeds and bring to fruition the efforts of centuries to reconquer the whole of Spain and humble the Moors. Isabella believed in doing one thing at a time. Every day she was increasingly convinced of the fact that, as Ferdinand had said when the war began, it was necessary "to pull out the teeth of this Granada, one by one." Meanwhile Columbus would have to cool his heels.

Left: A view of Granada from the Libro de grandezas de España *(1548) of Pedro Medina. This city had a period of particular splendor under Arab rule. Between the 11th and 14th centuries it was inhabited by no less than 400,000 people. This last Arab stronghold in Spain surrendered on January 2, 1492, to the besieging forces of the Catholic Sovereigns.*

Above, across both pages: Wooden bas-reliefs of the choir of the cathedral of Toledo, carved in 1495, when the local bishop was Pedro Gonzáles de Mendóza. On the left is shown the attempted assassination of the Catholic Sovereigns at Malaga. On the right, Ferdinand and Isabella enter Almería. Below: Two Spanish churchmen— left, Cardinal Gonzáles de Mendóza; right, Archbishop Fonseca. The "Catholic Sovereigns" (a title conferred by Pope Alexander V), forced Pope Sixtus IV to give their government the right of choosing the high-ranking prelates of Spain.

A WEARY WAIT

The six years between 1486 and 1492 must have put the patience of Columbus to a difficult test. Both at Cordova and at Salamanca, to which the court moved and he followed, there was talk of nothing but the war against the Moors. No one took any interest in a mythical voyage of exploration beyond the seas. Queen Isabella turned the plan over to a commission for study, and the commission's opinion, made known only in 1490, was unfavorable.

Columbus, however, did not wait passively for a decision. He busied himself with looking for friends and supporters in strategic positions. Among these was Doña Beatrice de Bobadilla, Marquesa de Moya, Isabella's closest friend, who took it upon herself to remind the queen that Columbus was waiting and hoping for a positive decision. With his forthright ways, Columbus must have had a certain attraction for women. At this time he entered into a relationship with a girl considerably younger than himself, in her early twenties, Beatriz Enriquez de Araña, and she bore him the son, Ferdinand, who was destined to become his biographer. Little is known about her, and to the inevitable question as to why they did not marry, there is no reply. She is mentioned in Columbus's second will, drawn up in 1502, and in a codicil of 1506 he instructed his legitimate son Diego to make provision for her "as a person to whom I am in so great debt, and thus for discharge of my conscience."

As the war dragged on from year to year, Columbus fretted. In 1488 he went back, with his brother, Bartholomew, to Portugal, where he had conversations with King João II. But just as these seemed to be turning out to his advantage they were cut short by an unexpected event, the appearance at the mouth of the Tagus River of the explorer Bartholomew Dias. Since setting out a year before, Dias had rounded the tip of South Africa and sailed for some distance up the east coast of the Dark Continent. An eastward passage to India was open, and it was useless for Columbus and his brother to remain in Portugal any longer.

Opposite page,
from top to bottom:
A royal manuscript and a notice
of payment, the latter signed
by Columbus with the title
El Almirante (*The Admiral*).
Both documents are in the
Archives of the Crown
of Aragon in Barcelona.
Columbus left on his
great voyage with a Latin
"passport," in which
the King and Queen said
that they were sending
him "*in the direction of
India*" (ad partes Indiae). *He
carried with him, also, three
identical letters of introduction.
One was addressed to the
Great Khan (emperor of China),
while the others had blank
spaces that Columbus was*
*to fill in with the titles of
any potentates he might
meet. Below:* Columbus
Setting Forth His Ideas
at the Monastery of
La Rábida (*Naval Museum
of Barcelona*). *The
prior, Fra Juan Pérez,
was Columbus's
faithful friend and
stalwart supporter.*

In the two engravings at the right: Columbus appearing before the scholars and the Royal Council. *Below:* Columbus at Salamanca by Barabino (Collection of the Contessa d'Albertis, Genoa). The commission appointed by Queen Isabella in 1486 was headed by her confessor, Fra Hernando de Talavera. Among the members was a loyal friend and admirer of Columbus, the Dominican monk Diego de Deza, professor of theology at Salamanca's St. Stephen's college, who was later to be archbishop of Seville. The scholars took four years to reach a decision, which was negative.

NO HELP
FROM THE
"SCHOLARS"
OF THE TIME

After their last attempt to find support in Portugal the Columbus brothers returned to Spain. Bartholomew set out for England, where he hoped to interest the parsimonious Henry VII in the project. He planned, if his efforts were in vain, to stop on the way back to speak to Charles VIII of France. His trip was much longer than expected, because on the way to England he was captured by pirates and held for some time as a prisoner.

Meanwhile, in the Dominican college of Saint Stephen, a part of one of the most famous universities of old Europe, the commission set up by the Queen in 1486 concluded its labors. It was what we would call today a "top-level" group, composed of learned men in various fields. There were friends of Columbus among them, but the project was turned down.

The adverse opinions came, really, from previous centuries. For the great doctors of the Church such as Augustine and Lactantius had opposed Columbus's theories in advance. The learned men gathered at Salamanca acted in accord with ecclesiastical doctrine and their own consciences. They pitted Columbus against the saints, and it was natural that the saints should win. Actually, although the scholars were mistakenly bound to the past, Columbus's certainties were not free of error. For one thing, he calculated the size of the earth and hence the breadth of the oceans as much smaller than they really are. Of course, it was this miscalculation that gave him, quite providentially, the courage to conceive and carry out his great enterprise. While the commission was debating, Columbus did, at least once, see the Queen. After that he continued to wait, until he made up his mind to join his brother, Bartholomew, in France. He went to La Rábida, presumably to fetch his son, as if he meant to leave Spain forever. And here Fra Juan Pérez re-enters the picture. In all probability La Rábida was the scene of a sort of council of war among Columbus's friends, including Fra Antonio Marchena and García Hernández, the doctor. Father Pérez wrote to the Queen about Columbus's intention of leaving Spain, and she sent an immediate reply, bidding him to come to court.

29

THE QUEEN'S JEWELS

The court was present at the siege of Granada. Headquarters were in Santa Fé, a walled and towered city that the Queen had built, in record time, after a raging fire had destroyed the Christian encampment. Columbus came to Santa Fé around Christmas of 1491, when the prospect of a quick victory had put everyone in good spirits. A new commission, in deference to the unstated but implicit will of the Queen, gave a less unfavorable opinion of Columbus's project. On January 2, 1492, Granada surrendered, and the war came to an end. Columbus witnessed the triumphant entry of Ferdinand and Isabella into the conquered city. Talk of the voyage was revived. The Queen herself made the final decision, pledging the support of the crown of Castile, even if it meant pawning her own jewels. The financing of Columbus's expedition was actually negotiated, in large part, through Italian banking interests in Spain.

Half of the two million *maravedis* ($14,000) was put up by Genoese and Florentine friends of Columbus, the other half by Luís Santángel and Francisco Pineli, joint treasurers of the *Santa Hermandad*, a sort of military brotherhood which defended the Crown. Pineli was actually from Genoa. Three-quarters of the sum (or, if we count Santángel a mere go-between, the whole of it) necessary for the expedition that was to give Spain a world empire was of Italian origin.

The Surrender of Granada, *in a painting by F. Pradilla. The Moorish king, Boabdil, came to the Spanish camp and turned over the keys of the city to King Ferdinand with these words: "Sir, here are the keys of your Alhambra and your city. Go, sir, and take them over." Ferdinand gave the keys to Isabella, who answered, bowing her head: "Everything is Your Lordship's."*

FRONTESPIZIO DEL LIBRO
FRONTISPIECE OF THE BOOK

STEMMA DI CRISTOFORO COLOMBO
CHRISTOPHER COLUMBUS'S COAT OF ARMS

A DRAMATIC CLASH OF WILLS

Left: Copy of the Book of Privileges (Titles) conferred upon Columbus by King Ferdinand and Queen Isabella (Naval Museum of Pegli). In the center is the coat of arms of the Admiral of the Ocean Sea. Beneath the emblems of Castile and León are some scattered islands and some anchors, symbolic of Columbus's prowess as a navigator. He was accorded one-tenth of the value of the gold, gems and other merchandise that it was hoped would be obtained from "The Indies." The search for gold was one of the major motives of the whole expedition. Columbus speaks of it often in his reports, perhaps because of all the trouble brought upon him by the Spaniards' lust for gain. Above: Two depictions of Columbus's last audience with the Queen; left, an anonymous painting, and right, one of the panels on the bronze door of the Capitol, Washington, D.C., dedicated to the discoverer of America.

Columbus's troubles were not yet over. But this time the difficulties were of his own making. Because he was so sure that his voyage would bring great riches to Spain, he wanted to receive adequate compensation. Perhaps he had the support of his financial backers, for Italian businessmen played an important role in Spain. Columbus asked for a tenth of all the profits obtained from whatever lands he might discover. Since no one had an exact idea of all that this implied, it is probable that the King and Queen held out not so much against his monetary claims as against the titles that he demanded. He demanded that, if all went well, he and his descendants be given the titles of Admiral of the Ocean Sea and of Viceroy and Governor of the newly discovered lands, with all the privileges proper to these positions. Moreover, he reserved to himself the right to choose the persons who were to hold administrative and judicial offices under him. These demands were, quite rightly, considered exorbitant, and negotiations were broken off. Columbus mounted his mule and rode off toward La Rábida. This time he would leave Spain for good. It is hard to explain why, just when he was about to reap the reward for his long patience, he should have given in to a moment of anger. Probably the humiliations that he had endured for so long had built up in him a sense of outraged pride. But a few miles from Granada a messenger overtook him and asked him to return. What had happened? It seems likely that Santángel and the Archbishop Diego de Deza, tutor to Don Juan, had intervened on his behalf. "His Grace the Archbishop was responsible for my staying in Castile," Columbus wrote, "when I was on the point of going away." At the court he found the King and Queen in a quite different frame of mind. His conditions were accepted, and on April 17 the Articles of Agreements were signed.

THE GREAT VOYAGE BEGINS

The "adventurous fleet" that Columbus assembled on the Rio Tinto, at Palos de la Frontera, was composed of three ships. Two of these, the *Niña* and the *Pinta*, were furnished, in payment of a fine owed to the Queen, by the city of Palos. The *Niña* was originally the *Santa Clara*, but because it had belonged to a family called Niño it acquired the feminine form of this name. As such and as the Admiral's favorite ship, it passed into history. The third ship was leased by Columbus from a certain Juan de la Cosa, who stayed aboard as first officer. It was called *La Gallega*, because the owner was from Galicia, but it became, under the name *Santa Maria*, the flagship, with Columbus as its commander. Martín Alonso Pinzón was in command of the *Pinta*, with his younger brother, Francisco, as his second. Another Pinzón, Vicente Yañez, commanded the *Niña*, with the original owner, Juan Niño, second in command. This was the "fleet" which at dawn on August 3, 1492 weighed anchor in the Rio Tinto and sailed down to the island of Saltes, to wait for a favorable wind. At eight o'clock in the morning the wind came up, filling out the sails and causing the many-colored flags to flutter, and the fleet put out to sea. The total number of officers and men aboard was 87—39 on the *Santa Maria*, 26 on the *Pinta* and 22 on the *Niña*. Most of them were Basques and Andalusians, but there were some men from remoter parts of Spain and from other countries—a Portuguese, a Genoese and a Venetian. It had been no easy task to put the crews together.

On facing page: An astrolabe in use in Columbus's time. Left: The tiny fleet on the high seas. Above, top: Embarkation and Departure of Columbus from Palos, *a colored print from the painting by Ricardo Balaca. Directly above: Columbus among his sailors on the westward voyage, a 17th-century print.*

Grad	Hore	Min	☋	Grad	Hore	Min	Dies
1	12	3		46		35	
2		7		47		43	
3		10		48		44	
4		14		49	16	1	
5		17		50		10	
6		21		51		21	
7		25		52		31	
8		28		53		43	
9		32		54		55	
10		35		55	17	8	
11		39		56		22	
12		43		57		37	
13		46		58		54	
14		50		59	18	12	
15		54		60		32	
16		57		61		54	
17	13	1		62	19	21	
18		5		63		51	
19		9		64	20	27	
20		13		65	21	14	Dies
21		17		66	22	27	0
22		21		67	14	18	24
23		25		68	9	24	42
24		30		69	8	36	53
25		34		70	5	22	63
26		38		71	22	32	71
27		43		72	20	40	79
28		47		73	5	23	87
29		51		74	19	26	93
30		57		75	17	26	100
31	14	1		76	0	51	107
32		6		77	2	52	113
33		12		78	0	24	119
34		17		79	18	12	124
35		22		80	8	50	130
36		28		81	20	47	135
37		33		82	6	30	141
38		39		83	19	21	146
39		44		84	20	34	151
40		52		85	1	32	157
41		58		86	5	24	162
42	15	5		87	8	30	167
43		12		88	8	54	171
44		19		89	13	2	177
45		27		90	14	55	182

Tabula signoꝛ iferius scripta ostendit / q̃tum sol ascendit q̃libet dieꝛ q̃libet sig / incipiendi i·i·g̃ q̃ ascendi praeq̃ui̇d iuf / ordine hic imposita

Gradus	0 / 6		1 / 7		2 / 8		Gradus
	G	M	G	M	G	M	
1	0	29	11	52	20	27	29
2	1	47	12	17	20	39	28
3	1	11	12	39	20	5	27
4	1	35	12	59	21	3	26
5	2	59	13	19	21	19	25
6	2	23	13	35	21	24	24
7	2	47	13	55	21	39	23
8	3	11	14	15	22	44	22
9	3	35	14	33	21	55	21
10	3	58	14	43	22	3	20
11	4	21	15	12	22	11	19
12	4	45	15	30	22	20	18
13	5	9	15	48	22	28	17
14	5	33	16	6	22	35	16
15	5	57	16	24	22	42	15
16	6	19	16	42	22	48	14
17	6	42	16	59	22	55	13
18	7	5	17	16	23	0	12
19	7	28	17	33	23	5	11
20	7	51	17	49	23	10	10
21	8	13	18	5	23	14	9
22	8	36	18	22	23	18	8
23	8	58	18	36	23	22	7
24	9	21	18	51	23	25	6
25	9	43	19	6	23	27	5
26	10	6	19	20	23	29	4
27	10	27	19	34	23	30	3
28	10	48	19	49	23	32	2
29	11	10	20	1	23	33	1
30	11	31	20	19	23	33	0
	5 / 11		4 / 10		3 / 9		

A CLOUD SUFFICED TO GUIDE HIM

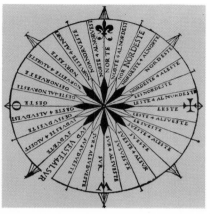

At sea Columbus was in his own element, "the greatest navigator of his age," as Samuel Eliot Morison calls him. Beside this enthusiastic judgment we may place that of one of Columbus's shipmates on the second voyage, Michele de Cuneo from Savona. "Ever since Genoa was Genoa," he writes, "there has been no such great-hearted man or keen navigator as the Admiral. He could tell from a cloud or a single star what direction to follow." In his previous voyages along the coast of Portuguese Africa Columbus had studied the play of the winds and plotted his route across the ocean. The north wind carried him to the Canary Islands, and it was from there that he struck out to the west. He had already noted that at this latitude (28.3° N.) there was a steady wind from the east and a generally calm sea, and his intention was to move westward straight along this parallel. He imagined that Japan was on the same parallel, 2,400 nautical miles away, and in his own words he defined his course as "neither north nor south, but west." If he had actually been able to stick to this plan he would have landed not at Guanahaní (which he renamed San Salvador, but is now known as Watling) but in Florida.

Above, top row, left to right: A Spanish ship, woodcut of 1496; Compass card from the Breve compendio de la sphera y del arte del navegar, *1551;* Mappa delle Maeriche *of F. Monachus, 1529. Bottom, left: The building of a ship, detail from a woodcut of 1486. Bottom, right: Various types of caravels, from the* Arte de navegar *of Pedro Medina. All these illustrations are taken from books that came out just before or after the voyages of Columbus. The compass card shows the four cardinal points of the compass and the intermediaries. At this time the points were called "winds."*

THE SAILORS
TAKE FRIGHT

The three caravels arrived at the Canaries on August 10 and did not set sail again until September 6, which was a Thursday. At dawn of the first day out they still lay becalmed between Gomera and Tenerife. At three o'clock Saturday morning there was finally a breeze, but until Sunday they did not lose sight of Ferro, the westernmost island of the archipelago. Many sailors, fearful of leaving these familiar places behind them, shed tears of apprehension. Martín Alonso Pinzón, a practiced navigator and something of a pirate, had persuaded many of them to join the expedition. "Come with us, my friends," he said. "Why go on living in poverty? We'll find houses roofed with gold tiles and come home laden with riches and glory." A materialistic argument, less inspiring to posterity perhaps than heroic or pious motives, but none the less effective.

Columbus was prepared to deal with his sailors' fears. He decided, from the beginning, to keep two counts of the distance covered every day, an accurate one for himself and a reduced one for the crews, "in order that," as we read in his Journal, "the men should not be discouraged or frightened by the excessive length of the voyage." He knew that he could count only on his own resolution. In a letter that he wrote on the eve of his departure and made the prologue to his Journal he proposed to "note down each night what that day had brought forth, and each day what was sailed by night." And he adds: "It is very important that I forget sleep and labor much at navigation. . . ." Yet, in spite of the obvious hardships of an ocean crossing in that century, the inevitable difficulties raised by a mixed and timorous crew and the later disloyalty of Martín Alonso Pinzón, the historic voyage was blessed by good fortune.

Above, left to right: Models of the Pinta, Santa Maria *and* Niña. *Below: a sea chest for stowing away clothing and a cabin such as that occupied by members of the crew (reconstructions in Barcelona). The name of "caravel" covered a variety of small ships, no more than 60-70 feet long and with a cubic capacity* of 60-70 tons. Portuguese and Andalusian shipyards specialized in caravel construction. During the stopover at the Canary Islands the Pinta underwent repairs and the so-called "lateen" rig of the Niña was transformed into a "square" rig.

"THE SEA WAS LIKE A RIVER"

"At this point the men complained that the voyage was too long and they could no longer endure it. The Admiral reassured the crew members as best he could, giving them hope of the gains that lay ahead and adding that their complaints were in vain because he was determined to reach the Indies and, with God's grace, would go on until he got there." With these words, jotted down in his Journal on October 10, Columbus refers to the incipient mutiny that he quieted. This episode has been variously depicted. Below: Columbus surrounded by his sailors. At the bottom of this page and on the opposite one: the sighting of land and the landing.

The 37 days (September 6–October 12) and 20 pages covered by Columbus's Journal give us a picture of steady winds on the stern and a calm sea. The weather was "like that of April in Andalusia," wrote Columbus on September 16. On September 26 he said that "the sea was like a river," and on October 8: "Thanks be to God, the air is mild, and so fragrant that it is a pleasure to breathe it." The gulfweed of the Sargasso Sea unrolled a green-and-yellow carpet before him, and later petrels, terns and pelicans flew over his ship, followed by field birds making their annual southward migration. Under the date of October 9 Columbus wrote: "All night long birds were flying over." The only trouble was the restlessness of the crews. Lurking terrors disturbed them—a meteor traversed the sky on the night of September 15 with "a marvelous streak of flame," and the trade winds blew so steadily from the east that, as Columbus says, it seemed that "in this sea there was no contrary wind such as to carry them back to Spain." All these things were causes of fear. On September 25 Pinzón thought that he had sighted land, and called out from the poop of his ship to Columbus: "Land, land, sir!" And he added, mindful of the prize that the King and Queen had promised to the first man to sight it: "I claim the reward!" Columbus fell onto his knees and they all sang the *Gloria in excelsis Deo.* But the "land" was a mere cloud formation, as it was to be again on October 7, when the *Niña* hoisted its flag and shot off a volley, the agreed signals of discovery. These two disappointments dampened the men's spirits. There were more and more signs of the nearness of land—a branch with flowers, a carved stick, and greater numbers of field birds. But, as Ferdinand Columbus writes, "so great were their desire and anxiety to sight land that they had lost all confidence in such omens" and "suspected that they had left some islands behind on either side, passing between them without noticing." Finally, Martín Alonso requested a change of route; Cipango (Marco Polo's Japan), he said, was southwest by west.

SAN SALVADOR

The change of route to which Columbus consented on October 7 was made in order to pacify the restless sailors and also because "a multitude of birds was seen flying from north to southwest, as if they intended to spend the night on land in the latter direction." Moreover Columbus "knew that most of the Portuguese island possessions had been discovered by following the flight of birds." On the evening of October 11, with an unusually heavy sea, Columbus shifted his course back to due west. At 10 o'clock, standing on the sterncastle of the *Santa Maria*, Columbus saw a light "like a little wax candle rising and falling." Doubting his own eyes, he called Pedro Gutiérrez, "butler of the king's dais" and a gentleman volunteer, who confirmed his impression. Then he called Rodrigo Sánchez of Segovia, the royal comptroller, who, however, saw nothing. At two o'clock in the morning land was clearly sighted by Rodrigo de Triana, a sailor aboard the *Pinta*, about six miles away. The sails were lowered and the ships drifted, at a safe distance from the breakers, for the rest of the night. The land was that of one of the islands of the vast archipelago, later known as the Antilles, extending between the Gulf of Mexico and the Caribbean Sea. In the morning they looked for an opening among the reefs, and found it on the west side. On the shore they saw a crowd of naked men, women and children, staring curiously at the white-sailed sea monsters. Columbus, together with Martín Alonso and Vicente Yáñez Pinzón, went ashore in an armed boat. They knelt down, kissed the ground and gave thanks to God. Columbus had with him the royal standard and the Pinzón brothers two banners on which were depicted a green cross and the initials of the King and Queen of Spain. In the presence of Rodrigo de Escobedo, secretary of the armada, Columbus took possession of the island in the name of the sovereigns. The island—one of the Bahamas—was called in the native tongue Guanahaní, but the Admiral rebaptized it San Salvador.

Left: Three woodcuts depicting scenes witnessed by the first Europeans to land on the shores of the New World. Extreme left: Indians taking flight before Columbus, from Dati's edition of The Letter of Columbus to the Sovereigns *of 1493. Center: A native craft, from* La historia del Mondo Nuovo *of Gerolamo Benzoni, who was there on the spot from 1542 to 1546 and whose book is a precious account of Spanish methods of colonization. Right: A 16th-century portrayal of cannibalism. Below: Frederick Kemmelmeyer's* Landing of Christopher Columbus (*Edgar William and Bernice Chrysler Garbisch Collection, New York*).

Below: Columbus Presenting Gifts to the Cacique of Haiti, *Venetian engraving of 1759. At the bottom of the page: Two illustrations from the* Historia general *of Antonio Herrera y Tordesillas (1549-1625); left,* Columbus Leaving a Garrison and Indians Killing the Spaniards; *right,* Arrival of the Cacique Guacanagarí at Navidad.

Of San Salvador, where he landed on October 12, 1492, Columbus said: "It is large and flat, with no mountains. There are green trees, much water and in the middle a big lagoon." The "lagoon" is the feature of the island that enables us to identify it as the Watling of today.

On this first voyage Columbus stayed for 96 days in the area of his discoveries. He sailed among the Bahamas, giving them names, mostly from the calendar of saints but including "Fernandina" (Long Island), "Ysabela" (Crooked Island) and "Juana" (Cuba). Everywhere he set up a cross. He came to Cuba in October and stayed in its neighborhood until December 4, exploring the coastline and the adjacent archipelagoes, and rowing up some of the rivers. Columbus went thus from marvel to marvel. But what about the gold, which was, after all, the object of his voyage and the lure with which he had attracted and held on to his followers? Except for a few small ornaments, which the natives readily exchanged for glass beads, tiny hawks' bells or other baubles, there was no gold to be found. The natives spoke of an island that they called Babeque (Great Inagua), "where . . . the people gather gold on the beach by candles at night." This was a false clue, but Martín Alonso Pinzón believed it, and sailed there with the *Pinta* on his own initiative. On November 21, Columbus noted this defection in his Journal. Apparently it was the latest of a series of misdeeds on the part of Pinzón, for it is written: "Many other things he had done and said to me." On December 6 the Admiral landed on Haiti, which so reminded him of Spain that he named it "Hispaniola." Here, on Christmas Eve, while Columbus was sleeping and the officer on watch had imprudently entrusted the tiller to one of the ship's boys, the *Santa Maria* went aground on a reef and had to be abandoned. Columbus chose to see in this event an indication of the will of Divine Providence. He left 39 men, now shipless, under the command of Diego de Haraña, to build a fort, which, in memory of the date of the accident, he called "Navidad." The men were also to explore the surrounding territory and to continue, of course, the search for gold.

Above: The shipwreck of the caravel Santa Maria *on the coast of Hispaniola, the modern Haiti. Far left:* The so-called Madonna of Columbus, *an anonymous painting. Near left: The construction of Fort Navidad, from* The Letter of Columbus *of 1493. In describing the beauties of Haiti, Columbus says that he was "of a mind to stay there indefinitely."*

45

A BRIEF HOUR OF TRIUMPH

*The triumphant return
of Columbus from his first
voyage was celebrated at
Barcelona. "All the court and
the city came out," says his
son's biography. His bearing was
compared to that of a Roman
senator. When he knelt down
to kiss the Sovereigns' hands,
they bade him rise and sit
in the place of honor, at
the queen's right hand. Among
the subsequent ceremonies
was the baptism of the
six Indians whom Columbus
had brought back with him.
To three of them the
King, Queen and Don Juan
acted as godparents. One was
even named Fernando de Aragon.
Another, named Don Juan de
Castilla, was the only one to
remain at the court, where he died
two years later. The others
went back with the Admiral to
"the Indies." The Sovereigns
had kindly feelings for the
Indians, but the benevolence
of the conquerors did not
last long. Within 50 years most
of their race—the Tainos—was
exterminated. Nor was the triumph
of Columbus long-lasting.
Less than three years later
Michele de Cuneo, a
companion of his second voyage,
wrote of the Spaniards and
their treatment of the Admiral:
"As long as Spain is Spain
there will be no lack of
traitors." Left: Robert Fleury's
famous painting of the
arrival of Columbus
at Barcelona (Luxembourg
Museum, Paris).*

47

Below: The Madonna of the Navigators (*a painting in the Alcázar of Seville*). *At the Madonna's right are King Ferdinand and Archbishop Fonseca; at her left Columbus, Vespucci and Vicente Yáñez Pinzón (a younger brother of Martín Alonso, who also took part in the first voyage).* Opposite page: above, left, a depiction of the legendary story of Columbus and the Egg (*a print made in Frankfort in 1590*); right, The Baptism of the Slaves Brought Back by Columbus (*a Venetian engraving of 1759*).

Columbus and everyone around him, including the King and Queen, were convinced that the success of the voyage lay in the discovery of a route to the Indies. There was no notion of any other land. The first person whose perusal of Columbus's accounts led him to develop a suspicion of the truth was an Italian humanist living in Spain, Peter Martyr (Pietro Martire d'Anghiera). In a letter he wrote in 1493 he coined the term "New World," which he used again in the title of an extensive work, *Decades de Orbe novo* (first printed in 1511). A realistic appraisal of the size of the globe, he said, made it unlikely that Columbus had really gone as far as Asia. But realization of the truth was slow in coming. Columbus himself believed to the end of his days that he had attained the goal he sought, that by sailing west he had reached islands off the coast of Asia and landed, to all intents and purposes, in the land described by Marco Polo.

Meanwhile, after considerable wandering, the *Pinta* also came back to Palos de la Frontera. The faithless Martín Alonso Pinzón fancied that he was the first to arrive and to bring news of the discovery to the Sovereigns of Spain. When he saw the *Niña* already in port, he had a heart attack and died. This is one version of his death, but there is another. According to that one he was the first European victim of an exotic disease, syphilis, a name pinned upon it in 1520 by Girolamo Fracastoro, a doctor from Verona. This disease, unknown in Europe, was widespread in the new world, where, with the passage of time, it had lost most of its virulence. When transmitted to the white race, it regained its original destructive power. "On that island (Hispaniola), such imprudent Spaniards as did not possess the virtue of chastity all caught it," says Bartolomé de Las Casas. Syphilis was rampant among the French soldiers whom Charles VIII led against Naples in 1494, and it was soon dubbed the French disease.

Below: Columbus Welcomed by Ferdinand and Isabella Upon the Return from His First Voyage (*detail from a painting by Ricardo Balaca*). On the return voyage Columbus ran into heavy storms. At one point, *fearing the worst, he wrote a brief account of his discoveries and ordered it enclosed in a barrel, which was cast into the sea.*

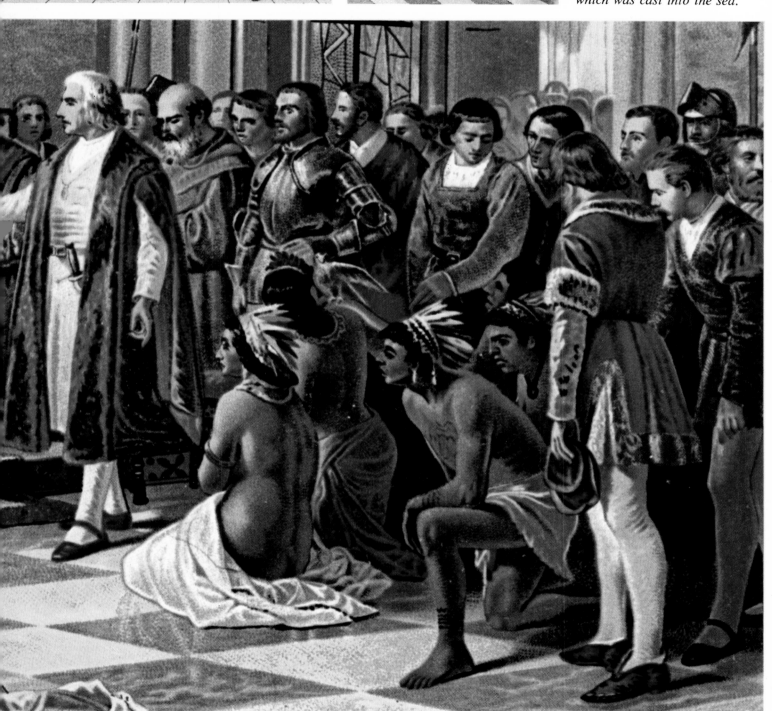

49

ADMIRAL OF
THE OCEAN SEA

From the Azores, on February 15, 1493, Columbus had written to Luís de Santángel an enthusiastic letter about his voyage, promising all sorts of things to the Sovereigns if they continued to help him: All the gold they could desire, spices, cotton, gutta-percha, aloes and any number of slaves, who were, he added, "idolaters." And, indeed, in the letter that the King and Queen sent to him they not only bade him come to be received at Barcelona but spoke of the preparations for another voyage as well. The letter was addressed to: "Don Cristóbal Colón, Admiral of the Ocean Sea, Viceroy and Governor of the Islands that he has discovered in the Indies." These were the titles that had been promised him a year earlier at Granada before he set sail. A few days before this the Sovereigns issued letters patent that established his right to a coat of arms. This coat of arms was privileged to include the castle of Castile and the lion of León, above the cluster of islands and the five anchors symbolizing Columbus's exploit and his admiralty, respectively.

Columbus stayed on for some weeks in Barcelona, through the celebrations of Pentecost and Corpus Christi. Meanwhile Don Juan de Fonseca, Archdeacon of Seville and nephew of the archbishop of the same name, was put in charge of preparations for the next voyage. Within a few months he assembled 17 ships, supplies for six months and some 1,200 men. During the same period the Sovereigns conducted territorial negotiations with the Holy See and with Portugal, whose interest in further exploration had been stirred by Columbus's success. Don João of Portugal had a more powerful navy than that of Spain, and it was necessary to share the Atlantic with him. Thus it was that Portugal later colonized Brazil. The Sovereigns' formal instructions for the second voyage were dated May 29, 1493. The primary object was stated to be the conversion of the natives, the secondary object the establishment of a trading colony. Columbus made a pilgrimage to Guadalupe and then joined Fonseca in Seville. On September 25, 1493, the "grand fleet" set sail. The flagship was another *Santa Maria*, formerly the *Mariagalante*.

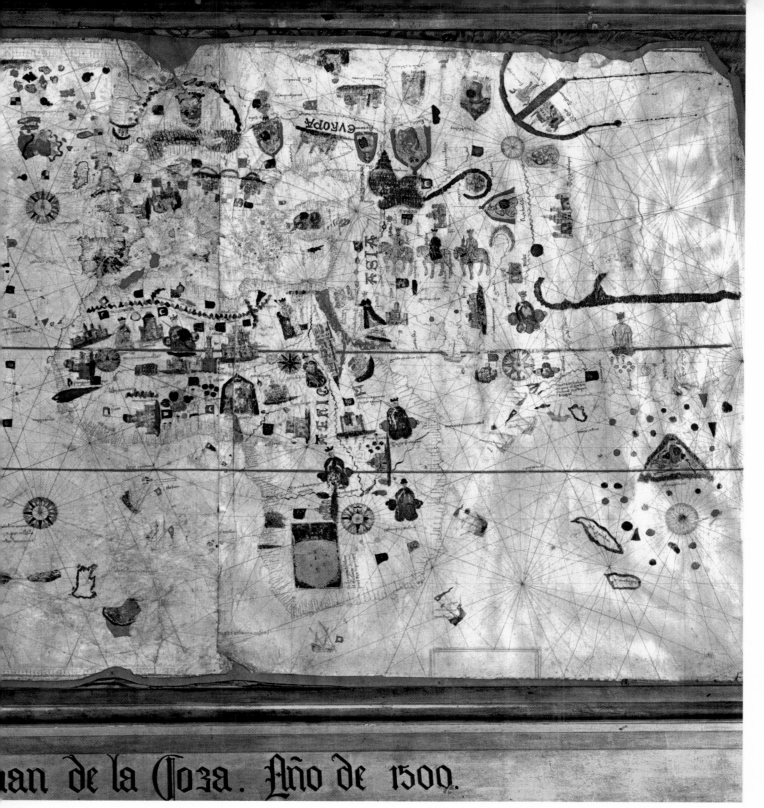

an de la Cosa. Año de 1500.

Above: the Carta de marear *or* Mapa Mundi *of Juan de la Cosa (1500). This precious map is the first on which the lands discovered by Columbus are considered as belonging to a new world.*

De la Cosa was a Spaniard who took part in the first two voyages of Columbus and in the voyage of Vespucci in 1499. Note, at the extreme left, the depiction of Columbus in the garb of St. Christopher. Below, left: a sketch, from

Columbus's own hand, of the northern part of Haiti, which he named Hispaniola (Archives of the Indies, Seville). Below, right: another drawing of Haiti from the 1516 edition of the Decades de Orbe novo *of Peter Martyr (Pietro Martire d'Anghiera).*

"A VERY HONORABLE MAN"

Center: Christopher Columbus on the Bridge of His Ship, *from a painting by Joaquín Sorolla y Bastida at the Mariners' Museum of Newport News, Virginia. Opposite page: Professional soldiers boarding ship for Columbus's second voyage, in a Venetian engraving of 1759 in the City Library of Milan.*

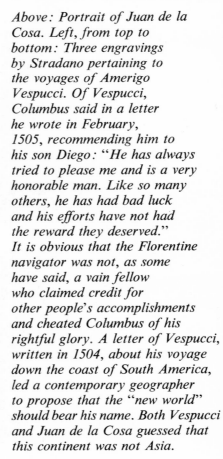

Above: Portrait of Juan de la Cosa. Left, from top to bottom: Three engravings by Stradano pertaining to the voyages of Amerigo Vespucci. Of Vespucci, Columbus said in a letter he wrote in February, 1505, recommending him to his son Diego: "He has always tried to please me and is a very honorable man. Like so many others, he has had bad luck and his efforts have not had the reward they deserved." It is obvious that the Florentine navigator was not, as some have said, a vain fellow who claimed credit for other people's accomplishments and cheated Columbus of his rightful glory. A letter of Vespucci, written in 1504, about his voyage down the coast of South America, led a contemporary geographer to propose that the "new world" should bear his name. Both Vespucci and Juan de la Cosa guessed that this continent was not Asia.

TROUBLE
IN PARADISE

The size of the grand fleet with which Columbus sailed from Cádiz bore witness to the importance given to this second expedition. The first land to be sighted, after 40 days at sea, was the island to which he gave the name of Dominica. Thence, island-hopping among the Lesser Antilles, Columbus made for Hispaniola. Halfway, on the island of Santa Cruz (St. Croix), a bloody battle was fought with the native Caribs. Charred human remains found in the huts of abandoned villages revealed the fact that they were cannibals. At Hispaniola Columbus suffered a grave disappointment, for the fort of Navidad was burned to the ground. Refusing to be discouraged, the Admiral founded another settlement, to which he gave the name of Isabella. Two months after his arrival at Hispaniola, Columbus sent 12 of his 17 ships, under the command of Antonio de Torres, back to Spain, to obtain further supplies for the new colony. With the five remaining ships, he explored the southern shores of Hispaniola and Cuba and discovered Jamaica, which he described as "the fairest island that eyes have beheld." When he returned, with his battered ships, to Isabella, he found there his brother, Bartholomew, who had come with three caravels loaded with supplies. The three caravels were taken back to Spain with a group of malcontents. In the autumn of 1494 Antonio de Torres returned, bringing more supplies. Columbus stayed on for a year and a half, until March 10, 1496, trying to curb the brutality and disorder that had begun to reign in Hispaniola.

FURTHER EXPLORATIONS

The two ships that Columbus took home—the *Niña* and the *India* (the latter built in Hispaniola with lumber from two other shipwrecked vessels)—arrived at Cádiz on June 11, 1496. Columbus went to meet the King and Queen at Burgos, wearing the habit of a Franciscan friar, which he did not put off until he died. The Sovereigns were kind enough, but he had a feeling that the old enchantment was broken. The third voyage was two years in preparation. Eight ships took part. The *Niña* and the *India* started out ahead in January, 1498, and sailed straight to Hispaniola. The other six were assembled at Sanlúcar de Barrameda and sailed on May 30. Three of them, carrying supplies, under the command of the devoted Alfonso de Carvajal, went from the Canaries to Hispaniola, while Columbus led the three others on a mission of further exploration. After touching the Cape Verde Islands, he went down to the zone of the equator and sailed west at a latitude of 9° 30′ N. After two months of navigation, at noon on July 31, he sighted the island of Trinidad, near the coast of Venezuela, in the area where the Orinoco River flows tempestuously into the Atlantic. Between Trinidad and the mainland there is a broad bay, the Gulf of Paria, where dangerous eddies are raised every day by the clash between the inflowing high tide and the outgoing rush of the river. Columbus entered the gulf at its south end and left it at the north. He was having trouble with his eyes and was afflicted with arthritis, and so, without being aware of the importance of his discovery of the continent, he went on to Hispaniola. Bartholomew had abandoned the unhealthy location of Isabella and founded a city on the west coast, on the bank of the Ozama River, which he named Santo Domingo. Winds and currents caused Columbus to overshoot the mark by a hundred miles. But he encountered a small ship in which Bartholomew was trying to overtake the little fleet commanded by Carvajal, which had also sailed by the new capital without stopping. Ten days later Columbus was at Santo Domingo.

Opposite page: Columbus executing Spaniards who rebelled at Hispaniola (from Americae Pars IV *of Th. de Bry, published at Frankfort in 1594). Above are two 18th-century Venetian engravings, illustrations of a book about Columbus. Top: A native girl enticing one of Columbus's soldiers. Bottom: Natives attacking a Spanish garrison.*

The engravings in the book of Th. de Bry depict episodes of Columbus's great adventure. Below, left: Natives forcing the gold-greedy Spaniards to swallow some melted gold. Right: Columbus and his brother Bartholomew arrested under orders from Bobadilla. Columbus in chains: Here is a subject that could not fail to inspire the imagination of painters and engravers. At the bottom of this page and on the next page are two prints from the Civica Raccolta Bertarelli *of Milan. In the small colored print we see, alongside Columbus, natives who remained faithful to him.*

THE CHAINS OF BOBADILLA

It was on August 31, 1498, that Columbus arrived at Hispaniola to find open rebellion. The leader of the rebels was Francisco Roldán, and their center of operations the coast of Xaragua, a long peninsula stretching westward in the direction of Jamaica. Here, by mistake, the little fleet of Carvajal had come to anchor, and he was unable to prevent his crews—among them many criminals—from joining forces with the rebels. He had to come to terms with Roldán, and on August 23, 1500, a commissioner especially appointed by the King arrived to investigate the situation. This was Francisco de Bobadilla, who belonged to the ancient knightly order of Calatrava and was a faithful servant of the Crown. At once he took over the governor's palace and listened to Columbus's enemies, who were all too ready to testify against him. He threw Columbus and his brothers, Bartholomew and Diego, into chains and ordered them back to Spain. Columbus, with his experience of Spanish justice, had reason to fear the worst. When Alonso de Vallejo came to escort him to the ship, he asked: "Vallejo, where are you taking me?" To which Vallejo replied: "Sir, Your Lordship is going aboard ship." Once they were under way, Vallejo wanted to remove the Admiral's chains, but Columbus would not let him.

Columbus lived in a brutal age, and the Spaniards could not help remembering that he came from a country other than their own. Nevertheless, his arrival in chains made a painful impression, especially upon the simple-hearted common people. As for Columbus, he never got over this humiliation. Not only did he continue to wear the Franciscan habit that he had put on at the end of his second voyage, but he kept the chains in his room and wanted them buried with him. This subject fascinated 19th-century painters. Above: Columbus's Departure in Chains from the New World, a panel by Randolph Rogers on the door of the Capitol in Washington, D.C. Right: Columbus Being Mocked, With Chains On His Feet. This painting by Lorenzo Delleani is at the Gallery of Modern Art in Genova-Nervi, a small town outside Genoa.

Below: King Ferdinand
Removes the Chains of Columbus,
*a painting by Emanuel Leutze
in the Bullard Collection,
Fairfield, Conn. As we have seen,
Columbus returned in chains
from his third voyage,
arriving at Cádiz toward the
end of October 1500. He was
received by the King and Queen
at Granada on December 17.*

HUMILIATION

Favorable winds speeded the Admiral's humiliating return. Before the end of October he disembarked at Cádiz and, still in chains, went to wait in the monastery of Las Cuevas at Seville for some word from the Sovereigns. Six weeks went by before orders came to free Columbus and his brothers from their chains. They were to present themselves at the Alhambra at Granada, where the Court was in residence. Columbus had written a long letter of self-defense to Doña Juana de Torres, a faithful friend at the Court. "I am here," he said, "and in such a state that even persons of the lowliest condition must despise me. Surely someone in the world will not allow this to be. If I had taken over the Indies and given them to the Moors I should meet no greater hostility." The letter is at the same time an outcry of sorrow and a proud defense of his achievement. Our Lord, he said, had made him a prophet of the "new heavens and a new earth." The Queen, to whom God had given understanding of his mission, had been chosen to inherit this new earth, and he had crossed the seas in her name to take possession of it. He had quelled two rebellions and defended the interests of the Crown. And then Bobadilla had heeded the slander of his enemies and thrown his brothers and himself into prison. Probably Isabella was told of this letter. In any case, Columbus's encounter with the King and Queen was friendly. They promised to restore his privileges and to see to it that justice was done. But their promises took no concrete form. Before this faithful servant who had given them an empire and then had been treated like a common criminal the Sovereigns were ill at ease. Months went by while Columbus tried in vain to settle his future. Finally the King and Queen, who were involved in European affairs, decided that the best thing would be to let him continue his explorations. A new governor had been sent to Hispaniola. On March 14, 1502, the Sovereigns authorized Columbus's fourth and last voyage. Two months later, on May 9, he set sail from Cádiz. The four caravels of his little fleet were the *Capitana* (the flagship), the *Gallega*, the *Bermuda* and the *Vizcaina*.

We have descriptions of Columbus thanks to the writings of his son and biographer, Ferdinand, and his shipmate, Juan de la Cosa. But there is no authentic portrait, in spite of the many unconvincing attempts, such as the one above, which is in the Uffizi Gallery in Florence. Above, left, between the two pages: Queen Isabella Receives Columbus Upon His Return From the Second Voyage, *print of a painting by Francis Jover. After the destruction of Navidad, Columbus founded a new town which he named Isabella in honor of his royal protectress.*

The itineraries of Columbus's four voyages, in the D'Albertis Collection in Genoa. I (above): The caravels Niña, Pinta and Santa Maria (flagship) sailed from Palos on August 3, 1492. They paused at the Canary Islands, whence they set out again on September 6. On October 12 they reached the island of San Salvador. Columbus explored Cuba and Haiti before starting home, with the Niña and the Pinta, on January 16, 1493. II (right): The second voyage began on September 25, 1493, and brought Columbus, in 39 days, to the Lesser Antilles. On June 11, 1496, Columbus returned to Spain, seeking to regain the confidence of Ferdinand and Isabella. III (below, right): Columbus embarked on the third voyage on May 30, 1498, touched Trinidad, came into sight of the continent of South America and made a landing near the mouth of the Orinoco. Subsequently he was arrested by Bobadilla and sent back to Spain in chains in October, 1500. IV (below, left): On May 9, 1502, with his son Ferdinand, Columbus sailed for the fourth and last time. He spent Christmas and New Year's Day of 1503 in Panama, little dreaming that the Pacific was only 35 miles away. He returned to Spain on November 7, 1504.

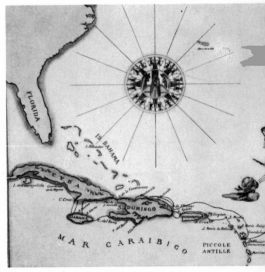

MONTHS OF SQUALLS AND HURRICANES

Columbus was 51, which at that time meant he was approaching old age. He suffered painful attacks of arthritis and had almost lost his sight. Yet he put out to sea again in the hope of discovering a strait between Cuba, which he thought of as China, and the continent he had discovered four years earlier in the Gulf of Paria. This, "the high voyage," as he called it, was the most adventurous of his undertakings. On June 29 he was off Santo Domingo, the new capital of Hispaniola, where the Sovereigns had forbidden him to disembark for fear he might enter into conflict with Don Nicolás Ovando, the new governor. The mouth of the Ozama River was crowded with a fleet of ships, commanded by Antonio de Torres, about to leave for Spain. Columbus asked and was refused permission to take refuge there in the face of an oncoming storm, and went to anchor in the nearby Rio Jaima instead. The homebound fleet imprudently set out the next day and was in large part wrecked by the hurricane that Columbus had predicted. Among the ships that went down was the one bearing Bobadilla and a cargo of gold. As for Columbus's ships, three of them were torn loose from their anchorage and carried out to sea, but four days later they rejoined the flagship without having suffered too much damage. Between mid-August and mid-September, while navigating along the coast of Honduras, Columbus ran into more storms, 28 continuous days of them. "The ships lay exposed to the weather," he wrote, "with sails torn, and anchors, rigging, cables, boats and many of the stores lost." Finally, at a point where the coast fell away to the south, a cape that Columbus named *Gracias a Dios* afforded protection. The caravels continued for several months to follow the coasts of Nicaragua, Costa Rica and finally Panama. The primary aim of searching for a strait gave way to a search for gold. The month of December was another period of fierce storms. And to the damage caused by bad weather was added the insidious boring of shipworms.

THE ADVENTUROUS RETURN FROM JAMAICA

Columbus reached the narrowest point of the Isthmus of Panama, where the two oceans are only some 35 miles apart. Here he spent Christmas of 1502 and the New Year's Day that followed. If he had gone in a small boat up the Chagres River, he would have beaten Balboa to the first view of the Pacific. Toward spring he started back eastward and landed on June 25, 1503 on Jamaica, where he stayed for a whole year. His two remaining ships were no longer seaworthy, but once they were beached they served as living quarters. Here, too, there was a rebellion; this was climaxed by a battle that, for lack of gunpowder, was fought with swords and won by the brothers Columbus. The natives, too, were restive, but the Admiral subdued them with an ingenious stratagem. Thanks to a German almanac of 1474 he predicted an eclipse of the moon and called it a sign of divine anger that he alone could bring to an end. Meanwhile two courageous men, Diego Méndez and Bartolomeo Fieschi, volunteered to travel by canoe the 100 miles to Hispaniola and there charter a rescue ship. The crossing of the "Windward Passage" was made in four days, but because of the ill will of the new governor, Ovando, it was 11 months before the rescue ship came, at the end of June, 1504. At Santo Domingo Columbus chartered another vessel and, on September 12, sailed for Spain.

On these two pages are three illustrations from the Americae Pars IV *of Th. de Bry concerning Columbus's last voyage. Above, left:* Spaniards and Monks Slaughtered by the Indians. *Above, right:* Ovando orders the Construction of a Caravel. *Opposite:* The Fight between Columbus and Francisco de Porras. *Nicolás Ovando went to take up his post in Hispaniola, with 2,500 men aboard a fleet of 30 ships, in 1502. A few months later he refused to allow Columbus to take refuge from the storm at Santo Domingo. During his governorship (1507-08) he treated the Indians with extreme cruelty and began the importation of Negro slaves. The De Porras brothers were equally fierce enemies of Columbus. Like Ovando, they hoped he would never return to Spain. One of them was captain of the* Santiago *and the other a Crown representative and comptroller. But their rebellion against Columbus and his brother Bartholomew was unsuccessful.*

Iamaica

Chriſtophorus Columbus

I4

MORE THAN
EVER ALONE

Columbus arrived at Sanlúcar de Barrameda after a rough, 56-day passage, on November 7, 1504. It was a sad return, of which hardly anyone took any notice. All attention was centered on the Queen, who lay mortally ill at Medina del Campo. She died 19 days after Columbus's arrival, on November 26, at the age of 53. For Columbus the loss was particularly grievous. Not that Isabella had been his never-failing protectress, but she had understood him, subscribed to his dream and tried, as far as she could, to facilitate his relations with her difficult husband. Now he was left, disarmed and alone, to cope with Ferdinand, who was not exactly faithful to his promises. Columbus was ill with arthritis, malaria and an inflammation of the eyeballs, and could not attend the Queen's funeral. But when he regained some of his strength he followed the court, which moved from one place to another, to Segovia, Salamanca and Valladolid. Ferdinand listened with apparent benevolence to his pleas for the percentages of colonial gains he claimed were owed him, but tried to persuade him to accept a grant of land in Spain and an assured income instead. Columbus stood firm and would take nothing other than what he thought was his due. His title of governor of Hispaniola was promised to his son Diego, now a member of the King's bodyguard, but he continued to press his own financial claims and to ask for the back wages of his sailors.

The Last Will and Testament of the Catholic Queen *by the Spanish painter Edoardo Rosales y Martínez (1836-73). While Columbus was sailing for the last time over the Ocean Sea to Spain, the Queen lay dying at Medina del Campo, and he was never to see her again. Columbus, too, was a sick man, old, tired and, above all, embittered.*

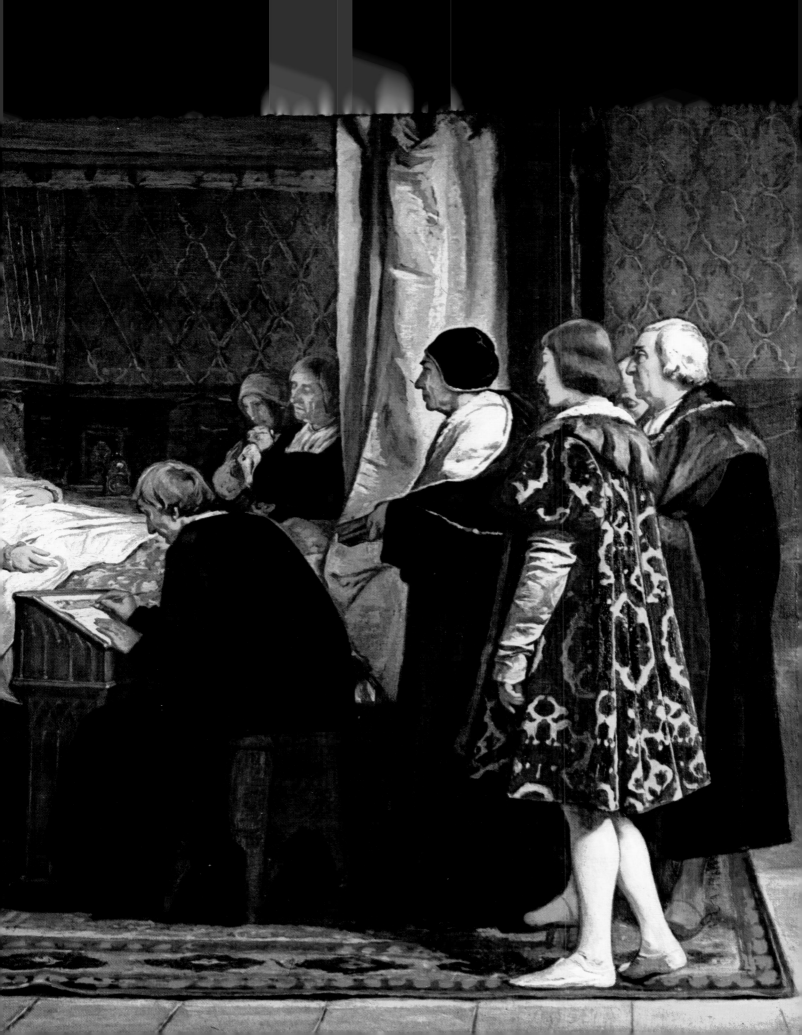

WHAT DID COLUMBUS REALLY LOOK LIKE?

One element of the so-called mystery of Columbus is that of his physical appearance. In spite of the many portraits and likenesses that bear his name, we do not really know what he looked like. We know that, at the beginning of his explorations, he already seemed older than his years. His son and biographer, Ferdinand, tells us that in his youth he was blond, but that at 30 his hair was white. The most authentic or at least most convincing portrait is that in the Gioviana Collection at Como, reproduced in color on the right, which was the basis of many others. Whatever may have been Columbus's physical appearance, we know that his manner was impressive. Ferdinand describes him as of more than average height, with an aquiline nose, blue eyes and a light complexion. A Portuguese historian, who was alive close enough to the time of Columbus to gather eyewitness accounts of him, says that he was "an eloquent speaker and a Latin scholar," also that he was "a man of proud bearing," a characteristic that we may link to the natural gravity described by his son. Certainly we cannot easily imagine Columbus as laughing. In the varied collection of likenesses on this and the next page he is almost always lost in thought.

"INTO THY HANDS I COMMEND MY SPIRIT"

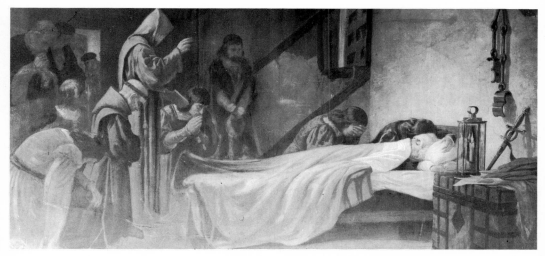

One day Columbus received a visit from Amerigo Vespucci, and recommended him to his son Diego. Later, in 1507, the geographer Martin Waldseemüller, in his *Cosmographiae universalis introductio*, suggested that the newly discovered lands be named America, in honor of the Florentine navigator. The Admiral could not protest, because for a year he had been buried under a stone in the Franciscan monastery of Valladolid, where he died on May 20, 1506. The day before, he signed his last will and testament, in which he named his son, Diego, as his main heir. Three years after his father's death Diego was made governor of Hispaniola. But he was involved in a long, drawn-out lawsuit against the Treasury, in which his half-brother, Ferdinand, was his supporter. Columbus must have had a feeling that Ferdinand was the better man of the two, for he wrote no less than three letters in his praise to Diego, in one of which he said: "Your brother, God be praised, is such a man that he will be very necessary to you."

Columbus took a rapid turn for the worse, and a priest was called to minister to him. With his last words he echoed those of Jesus: "Father, into Thy hands I commend my spirit."

Here we have the last hours of Columbus as depicted by Sciallero and Ortega. Opposite page: In the painting by Luigi Sciallero, Columbus holds, accusingly, the chains in which he returned to Spain from his third voyage. Present at Columbus's deathbed were his two sons and his brother Diego. At the right is a notary, intent upon taking down his last wishes. Columbus's principal heir was his son Diego. Above: The painting by Francisco Ortega is of the scene immediately following the death of Columbus. The next day was the feast of the Ascension, when church bells filled the air of Valladolid with their joyful ringing.

Below, left: The Glorification of Columbus, *a colored print.* *Below, right:* Columbus's tomb in the cathedral of Santo Domingo. Bottom of the page: *Sketch of a glorification of Columbus by the Genoese painter Lazzaro Tavarone (1556–1641). Opposite page: The urn with part of Columbus's ashes at the Palazzo Tursi in Genoa.*

Even in death the great navigator found no stable abode. From Valladolid, where he died, his ashes were taken first to Seville and then to Santo Domingo, whence they were brought back to Seville. Later, part of them was taken to Genoa and another part to the University Library of Pavia.

THE TRUE GREATNESS OF COLUMBUS

In recent years, the question of who really first "discovered" America has given rise to new controversy. There is a possibility that many peoples may have reached one of the American continents or islands before Columbus—ancient Phoenicians, Romans, and Chinese, a band of fifth-century Irish monks, the 12-century Welsh king Madoc, and, of course, the far-venturing Norsemen. For all except the last-mentioned, evidence is fragmentary and largely circumstantial. However, with the recent unearthing of apparent early Norse settlements in Newfoundland and the discovery of the 1440 Vinland Map, showing a large body of land to the west of Greenland, it may very well be the Norse were treading American soil long before Columbus was born.

But, for all the excitement of a mystery, the question is largely academic. The important fact is that Columbus led the first *successful* discovery. For it was followed immediately by further exploration and eventually colonization. By 1492 Europe was ready for America. There was a measure of political stability; a superior military and naval technology had been established; population pressure was beginning to build; and, most important, men's minds were ready to cast off medieval superstition and provincialism for the adventure of conquering new worlds.

Future discoveries may prove that some stray adventurer or storm-driven sailor did indeed reach American shores before Columbus. But none will ever dim the greatness of the courageous Genoese navigator, Admiral of the Ocean Seas, whose voyages changed forever the face of the world.

AN ALLEGORY OF THE GREAT DISCOVERY

Allegory of the Discovery of the New World *on the shield of Charles V (1519–1556) in the Royal Armory of Madrid. By the time of Charles V the importance of Columbus's discovery was fully recognized. All American countries are* planning *a joint project to build a monument to the discoverer on the south shore of Haiti (Hispaniola), where he said he was "of a mind to stay indefinitely." Here will rest the greater part of his mortal remains, now in Seville.*

1451—Born in Genoa, the son of a Ligurian weaver, Domenico. Isabella of Castile and (perhaps) Amerigo Vespucci born the same year.

1474—Columbus sails on an early trading voyage to the Greek island of Chios.

1476—He lands, after a shipwreck, on the coast of Portugal.

1477—He sails north, perhaps to Iceland. This first contact with the limits of the known world may have attracted him to the unknown.

1479—After a last return to Genoa he goes back to Lisbon. At this period he reads and makes revealing marginal notes in the *Imago mundi* of Cardinal Pierre d'Ailly, the *Historia rerum ubique gestarum* of Pius II Piccolomini and the *Book of Ser Marco Polo*, all of which further stimulate his curiosity and ambition. Probably in this same year he marries Felipa Perestrello-Moniz, who was related to the Portuguese royal family. He goes to live at Porto Santo, a small island near Madeira, where he is enthused by the study of the maps of his deceased father-in-law and rumors of carved wooden objects swept up by the sea.

1480 or 1481—Birth of his son Diego.

1486—First meeting, at Cordova, with Ferdinand and Isabella, after vain attempts to win support for his projected explorations from João II of Portugal. The Portuguese king was interested in the circumnavigation of Africa and the discovery of an eastward rather than a westward route to the Indies.

1487—Bartholomew Dias rounds the Cape of Good Hope.

1488—In Cordova, Columbus, who was left a widower, probably in 1483, enters into a relationship with Beatriz Enríquez de Haraña, out of which is born his son Ferdinand, later a humanist, man of science and his father's biographer.

1492—January 2: The capture of Granada, the last Arab stronghold in Spain. August 3: Columbus sails from Palos. October 12: He lands on an island of the Bahamas, to which he gives the name of San Salvador. October 28: Discovery of Cuba.

1493—March: Columbus is triumphantly received upon the return from his first voyage. September 25: Start of the second voyage (17 ships, 1,200 men). He sights land early in November and for the rest of the month sails from island to island (46 of them) of the Lesser Antilles.

1494—May-September: Exploration of Cuba. June 7: Treaty of Tordesillas, which pushes farther west the dividing line between Spanish and Portuguese zones of influence.

1496—June 11: Columbus's return from the second voyage. He defends himself against the accusations of the rebels of Hispaniola.

1497-98—The Venetian John Cabot, in the employ of England, discovers Labrador, Newfoundland and Nova Scotia.

1498—May 18: Vasco da Gama lands at Calicut (Kozhikode), India, after rounding the Cape of Good Hope and crossing the Indian Ocean. May 30: Start of Columbus's third voyage; some of the crew members were convicts. Discovery of Trinidad and the Gulf of Paria, landing at the mouth of the Orinoco River. Meanwhile there are grave disorders in Haiti.

1499—Hojeda, Juan de la Cosa and the Florentine Amerigo Vespucci explore Venezuela.

1500—August 23: Bobadilla, sent to investigate the troubles in Haiti, arrests Columbus. The discoverer of the West Indies returns in chains to Cádiz. December 17: Columbus is received by the King at Granada. He retires to a monastery, where he draws a map of the new lands. He has an idea that they are a barrier in front of Asia and wants to go back to find a passage. Cabral discovers Brazil, which, by virtue of the Treaty of Tordesillas, becomes Portuguese colony.

1501—Amerigo Vespucci, in the service of Portugal, sails down the whole coast of Brazil.

1502—May 9: Columbus sets out for the fourth time, with four small ships. June 15: He reaches Martinique, sails to Honduras and goes as far as Panama, within a few miles of the Pacific Ocean.

1504—November 7: return from the fourth voyage. November 26: death of Queen Isabella.

1506—May 20: Christopher Columbus dies at Valladolid.

1507—In a treatise of the German geographer Waldseemüller the name of "lands of Americo" is given to the discoveries of Vespucci.